2ND EDITION

TECHNIQUE & ARTISTRY BOOK

LEVEL **2A**

PIANO

Adventures® *by Nancy and Randall Faber*
with Victoria McArthur

THE BASIC PIANO METHOD

Note: All exercises and pieces are by
Nancy and Randall Faber unless otherwise noted.

FABER
PIANO ADVENTURES®
3042 Creek Drive
Ann Arbor, Michigan 48108

The student should learn these five *Level 2A* "technique secrets" gradually. The secrets are referenced one by one in the *Piano Adventures® Lesson Book*. (Correlating pages are shown at the bottom of the page.)

The teacher should demonstrate each "technique secret" as it is introduced.

Five Technique Secrets

1. **The first secret is FIRM FINGERTIPS.**

Exercise: Finger Inspector
(on the closed keyboard lid)

- Place your **right hand** in a **round** hand position.

- Use your L.H. 2nd finger and lightly press each R.H. fingernail.

  Did you pass inspection by keeping **firm fingertips**?

- Now repeat with your **left hand** in a round hand position. (Your R.H. 2nd finger will inspect your L.H. fingertips.)

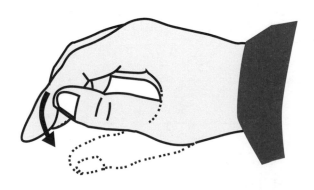

2. **The second secret is a LIGHT THUMB.**

Exercise: Light as a Feather
(on the closed keyboard lid)

- Place your R.H. in a round hand position.

- Rest fingers 2, 3, 4, and 5 on their fingertips, and lightly tap this rhythm with the *side tip* of your **thumb**.

Whisper: "Thumb is play-ing light-ly."

- Now repeat *Light as a Feather* with your L.H. in a round hand position.

3. The third secret is FAST FINGERS.

Exercise: Flying Fingers
(on the closed keyboard lid)

A pianist must be able to play **finger patterns** quickly.

- Practice this **finger pattern** with your R.H. on firm fingertips.

$$\| : \quad 1 \; - \; 3 \; - \; 2 \; - \; 4 \quad : \|$$

"Play" 4 times SLOWLY, *forte*.
"Play" 4 times QUICKLY, *piano*.

- Now repeat with your L.H.

4. The fourth secret is HANDS-TOGETHER COORDINATION.

Exercise: Team Players
(Play in the C 5-Finger Scale.)

Practicing **hands together** is like a sports team "in training."

- Practice this pattern **HANDS TOGETHER** in the C scale. Your fingers will be playing in contrary motion.

$$\| : \quad 1 \; - \; 2 \; - \; 3 \; - \; 2 \; - \; 3 \; - \; 4 \; - \; 5 \quad : \|$$

- Play 4 times SLOWLY, *forte* to train the fingers.
- Play 4 times QUICKLY, *piano*.

5. The fifth secret is a WRIST FLOAT-OFF.

Exercise: Moon Walk
(with damper pedal down)

Pretend you are walking on the moon.

- Play a Middle C on the piano with **R.H. finger 3**.

- Let your wrist rise in s-l-o-w m-o-t-i-o-n (float-off) and land gently on each HIGHER C. Keep a slow, steady rhythm.

- Repeat with **L.H. finger 3** moving down the keyboard playing C's.

Parallel Motion: Hands-together playing with notes moving in the SAME direction.
Are the first two exercises in parallel motion?

Technique Secret:
firm fingertips

Warm-up with *Finger Inspector* (p. 2).

Travel Tips

- Play hands alone first.

- Play s-l-o-w-l-y **hands together**.

- Gradually work up to a faster tempo.

New York Taxi Ride

_____ **5-Finger Scale**

Running for the Taxi
Steadily

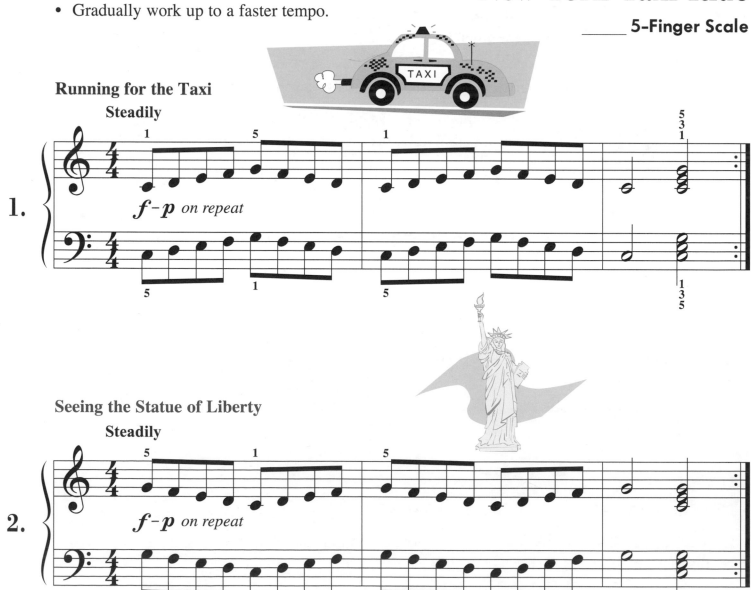

1. *f*-*p* on repeat

Seeing the Statue of Liberty
Steadily

2. *f*-*p* on repeat

  Lesson p.11 (Famous People) FF1098

Contrary Motion: Hands-together playing with notes moving in OPPOSITE direction.
The next exercise is in contrary motion.

Around Central Park

Steadily

3.

f-p *on repeat*

Down Broadway   Is this exercise in **parallel** or **contrary motion**?

Steadily

4.

f-p *on repeat*

Teacher Note: These exercises may be transposed as students learn new 5-finger scales.
The 12 major 5-finger scales and 7 white-key minor scales are shown on pp. 34–39.

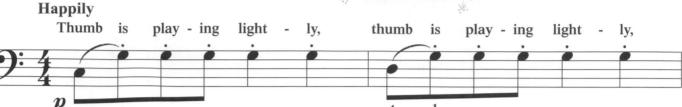

Technique Secret:
light thumb

Warm-up with *Light as a Feather* (p. 2).

Little Llama
(for L.H. alone)

Happily

Thumb is play-ing light-ly, thumb is play-ing light-ly,

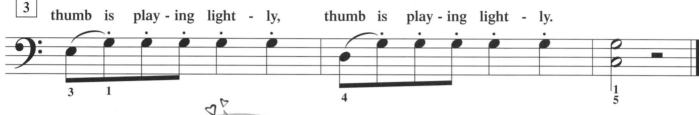

3 thumb is play-ing light-ly, thumb is play-ing light-ly.

Mama Llama

Happily

mp Thumb is play-ing light-ly, thumb is play-ing light-ly,

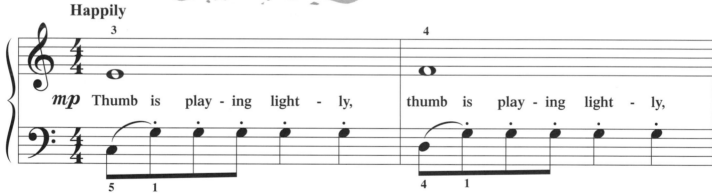

3 thumb is play-ing light-ly, thumb is play-ing light-ly.

Teacher Duet: (Student plays *as written*) Use for both exercises.

6 Lesson p.12 (Skip to My Lou)

FF1098

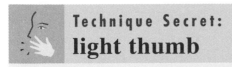
Thumb Check: Circle all the **B's** to ✏
remind you to play with a *light thumb*.

Thumb at the Gym
(for R.H. alone)

Faber, Faber, McArthur

Workout 1

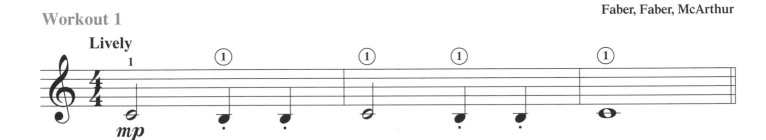

Workout 2

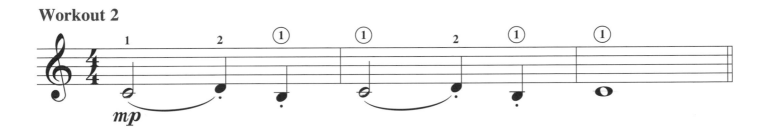

Workout 3

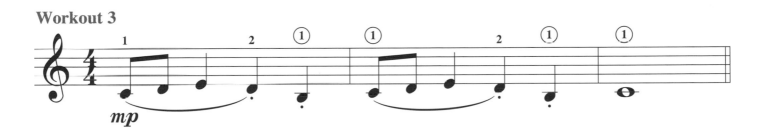

Workout 4

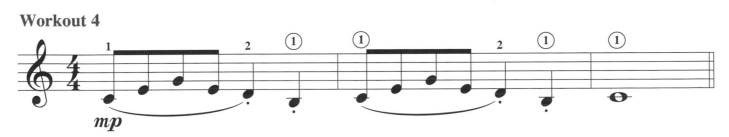

- Repeat *Thumb at the Gym* playing **one octave higher**.

Teacher Duet: (Student plays *as written*) Use for Workouts 1, 2, 3, and 4.

Play 4 times!

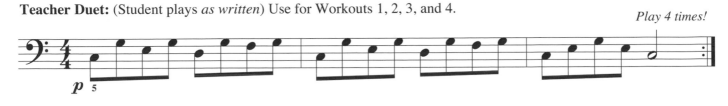

Every piece has a mood.

- What is the mood of *Race Car Rag*?
- Put a ✔ next to the best answer. ✏️

    _____ sad   _____ wild and fast

    _____ mysterious   _____ lazy

    _____ calm   _____ sweet and gentle

Race Car Tips

- First practice at a s-l-o-w tempo (speed).
- Then gradually working up to a "winning speed!"

Race Car Rag

N. Faber

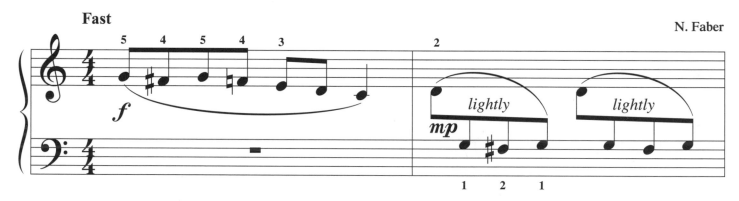

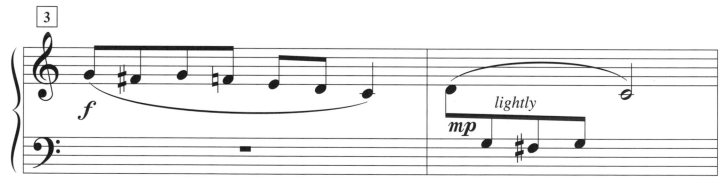

Teacher Duet: (Student plays 1 octave *higher*)

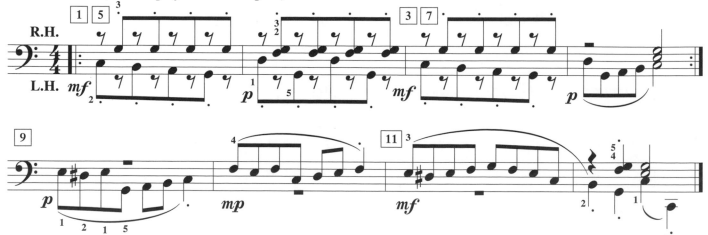

8   📖 Lesson p.16 (Mr. Brahms' Famous Lullaby)   FF1098

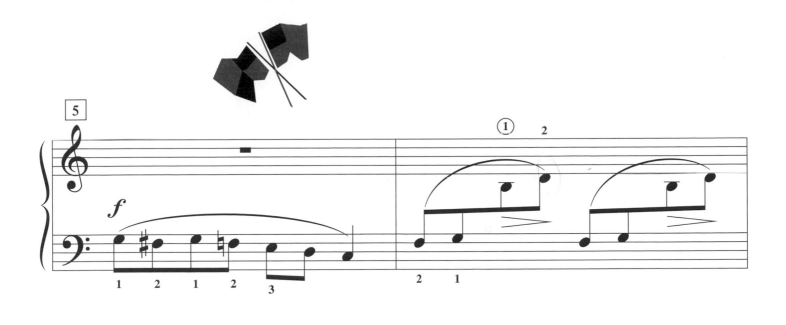

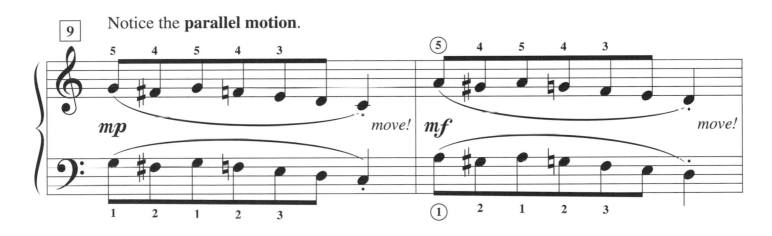

Notice the **parallel motion**.

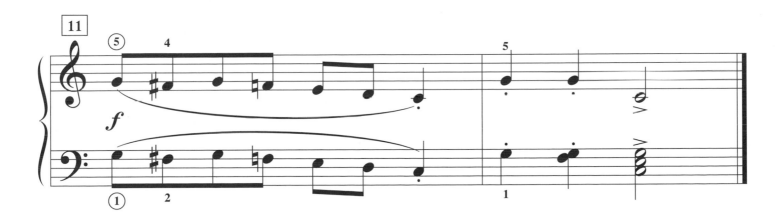

Technique Secret:
fast fingers

Warm-up with *Flying Fingers* (p. 3).

- Can you make it through the "1st stage" without an error?

Video Game

1st stage: C 5-Finger Scale

Rather fast

I can play the first stage, I can play the first stage,
mf
1 3 2 4 3 5

I can play the first stage, I can play the first stage. Score points!
1 3 2 4 3 5

- Now try the "2nd stage" without an error!

Video Game

2nd stage: G 5-Finger Scale

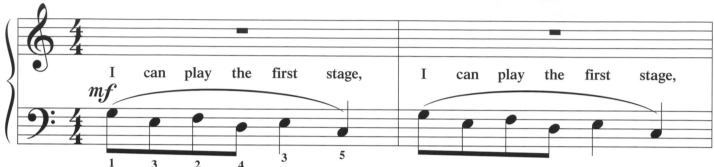

Rather fast

Sec-ond stage is eas-y, Sec-ond stage is eas-y,
mf
1 3 2 4 3

Sec-ond stage is eas-y, Sec-ond stage is eas-y. Score points!
1 3 2 4

Lesson p.18 (Ice Cream, More Ice Cream)

FF1098

Technique Secret:
hands-together coordination

Warm-up with *Team Players* (p. 3).

Schools of Fish
G 5-Finger Scale

Hold the damper pedal down for an underwater effect!

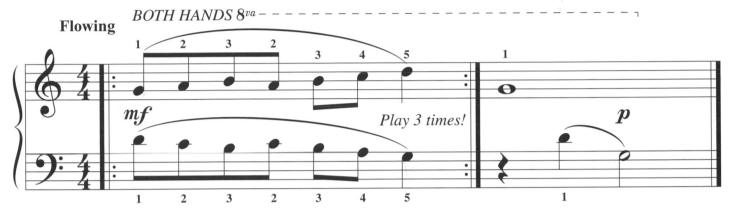

- Transpose to the **C 5-finger scale**.
  Notice that your hands are playing in
  contrary motion.

- Hint: First practice s-l-o-w-l-y.
  Listen for **steady rhythm.**

- Then play lightly, at a quick speed!

The Sandpiper
G 5-Finger Scale

Ti - ny beach bird run - ning quick - ly,

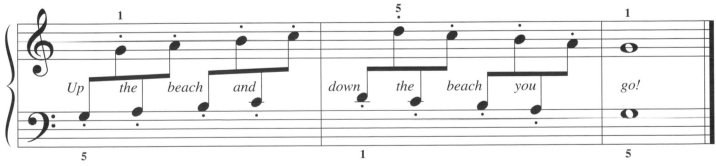

Up the beach and down the beach you go!

- Transpose to the **C 5-finger scale**.

Play *The Sandpiper* in the lowest **G 5-finger scales**.

Can you give it a new title? _____

Crescendo and ***diminuendo*** are important tools for playing with expression.

- As you play each *crescendo* and *diminuendo* in this piece, imagine the changing colors of the sunset.

Colorful Sunset

_____ **5-Finger Scale**

Hold the damper pedal down throughout the piece.

N. Faber

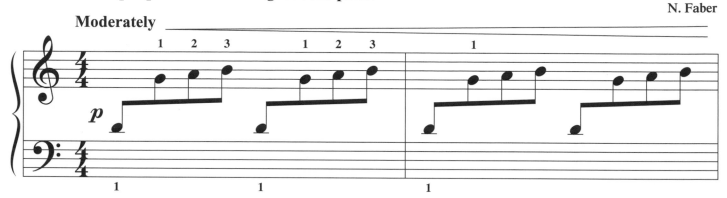

Teacher Duet: (Student plays 1 octave *higher*) Teacher pedals with duet.

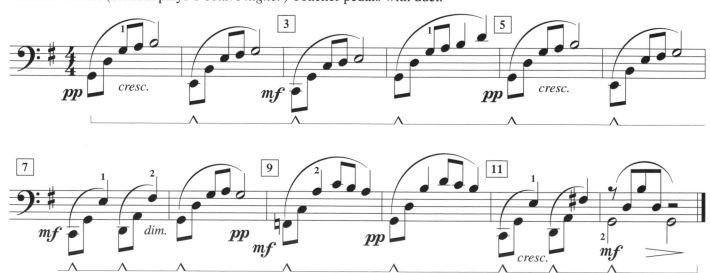

📖 Lesson p.22 (The Clock Strikes Thirteen!)   FF1098

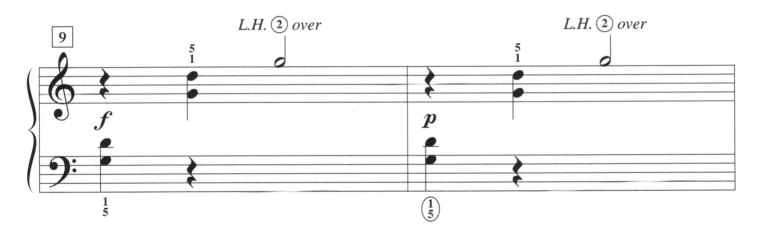

 Can you transpose *Colorful Sunset* to the **C 5-finger scale**?

Shaping the Phrase

- When we speak a sentence, our voice rises and falls with expression. Musical phrases also rise and fall.

- We can "shape a phrase" with small *crescendos* and *diminuendos*. A relaxed wrist will help you "shape" beautiful phrases.

 Technique Secret: wrist float-off

Warm-up with *Moon Walk* (p. 3).

Famous Phrases
(for R.H. alone)

Optional: Circle the $<$ and $>$ signs with a colored pencil as a reminder to "shape" each phrase.

Silent Night

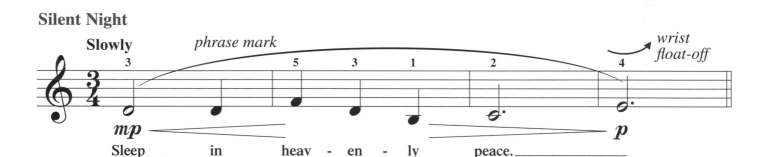

Scarborough Fair

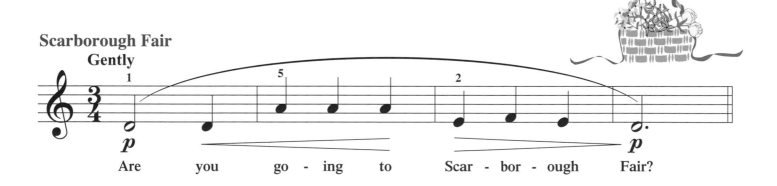

Joshua Fought the Battle of Jericho

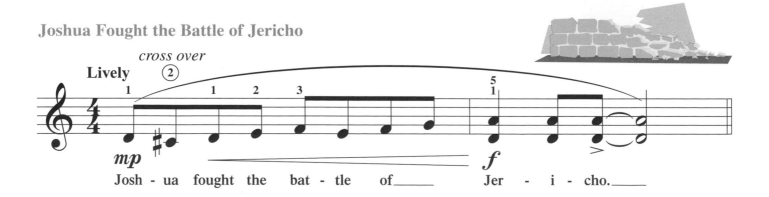

Technique Secret:
wrist float-off

Warm-up with *Moon Walk* (p. 3).

Famous Phrases
(for L.H. alone)

Optional: Circle the ‹ and › signs with a colored pencil as a reminder to "shape" each phrase.

The Riddle Song

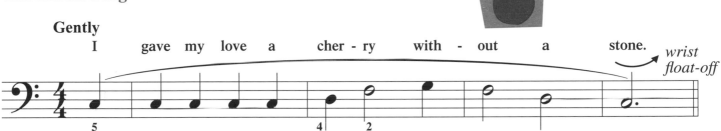

For Hc's a Jolly Good Fellow

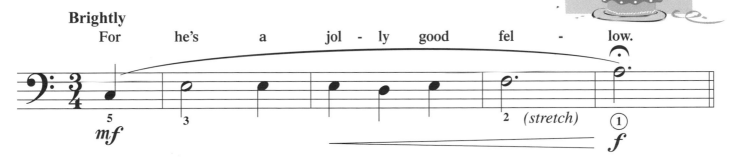

The Snake Charmer

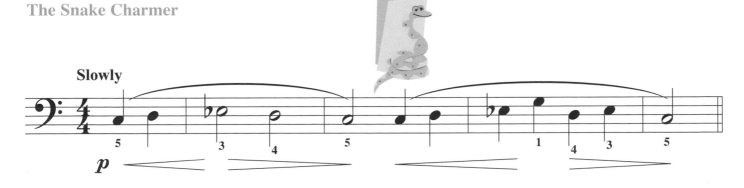

- As you learn this beautiful folk song, play more than "just the notes." Shape each phrase with *crescendos* and *diminuendos*.

The Riddle Song

Moving expressively

American folk song

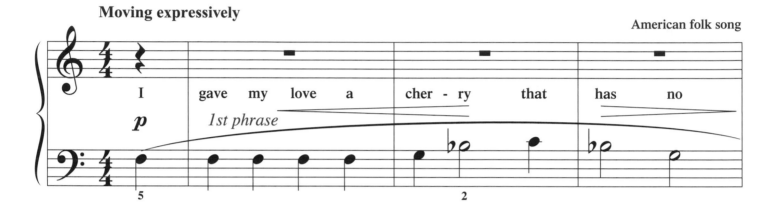

I gave my love a cher - ry that has no

p   *1st phrase*

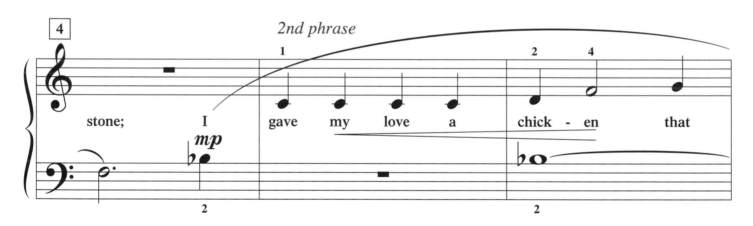

stone; I gave my love a chick - en that

2nd phrase   *mp*

Teacher Duet: (Student plays 1 octave *higher*)

R.H.

L.H. *with pedal*   *pp*

p

p   *p*   *mf*   *dim.*

p   *p*   *pp*

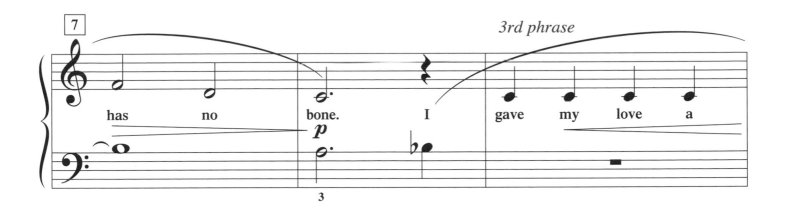

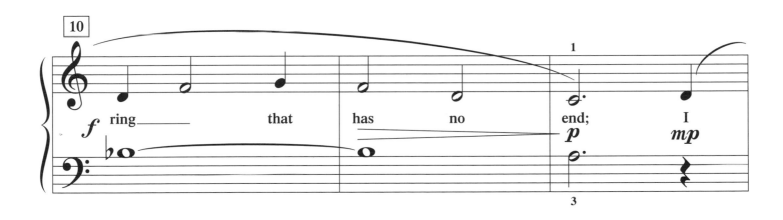

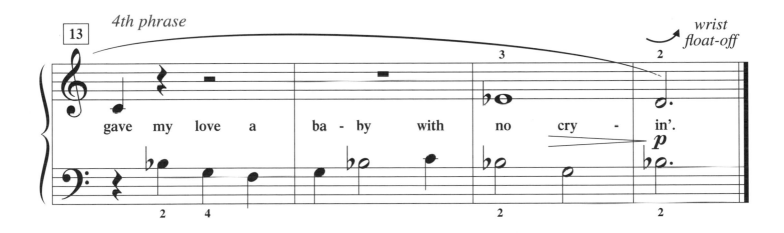

Additional lyrics

2. How can there be a cherry that has no stone?

   How can there be a chicken that has no bone?

   How can there be a ring that has no end?

   How can there be a baby with no cryin'?

3. A cherry, when it's blooming, it has no stone;

   A chicken, when it's pipping, it has no bone;

   A ring, when it's rolling, it has no end;

   A baby, when it's sleeping, there's no cryin'.

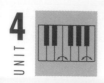

Technique Secret:
firm fingertips

Warm-up with *Finger Inspector* (p. 2).

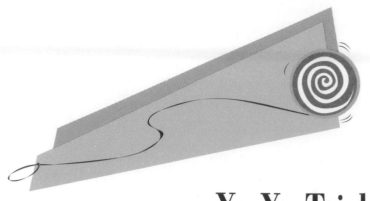

Yo-Yo Trick
(for R.H. alone)

McArthur

• In this half-step exercise, use **finger 3** to play the **black keys**. Remember to play on the *side tip* of the thumb.

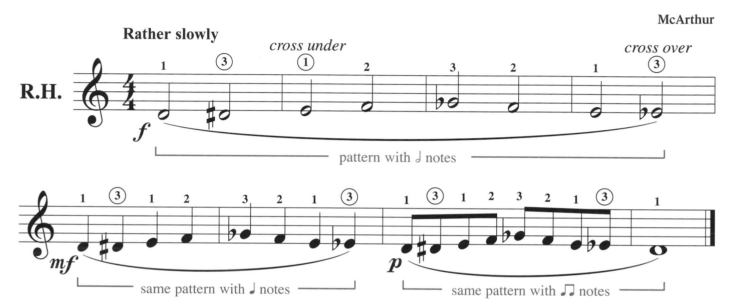

• Yo-Yo Stunt: Play the exercise in a *higher* octave.

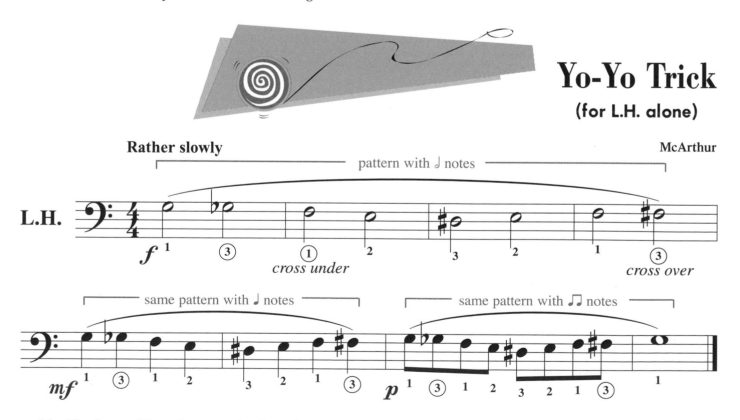

Yo-Yo Trick
(for L.H. alone)

McArthur

• Yo-Yo Stunt: Play the exercise in a *lower* octave.

- In this **whole-step** piece, your hands must travel smoothly up an octave at *measures 6* and *15*.

- Use a wrist float-off for a "smooth ride."

Star Traveler

Hold the damper pedal down throughout the piece.

Music by N. Faber
Lyric by C. Bowman

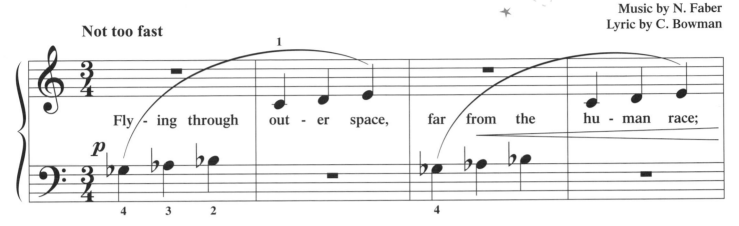

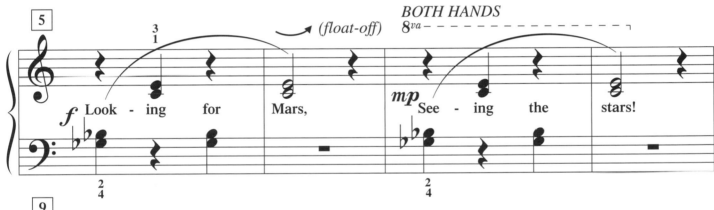

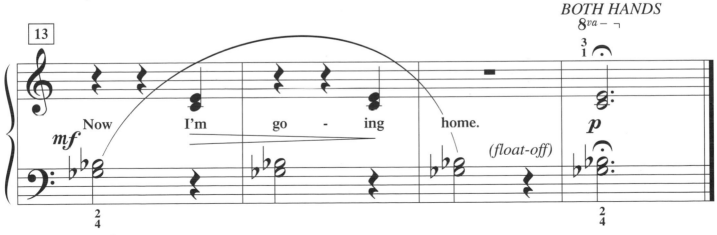

Sound Check: Did you play each *crescendo* and *diminuendo*?

Lesson p.30 (Our Detective Agency)

Technique Secret:
wrist float-off

Warm-up with *Moon Walk* (p. 3) on D's.

Around the World

D 5-Finger Scale

Over the Atlantic

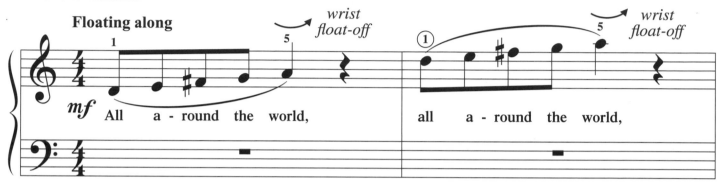

All a-round the world, all a-round the world,

Over the Pacific

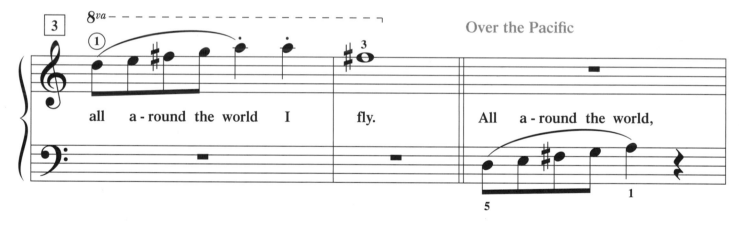

all a-round the world I fly. All a-round the world,

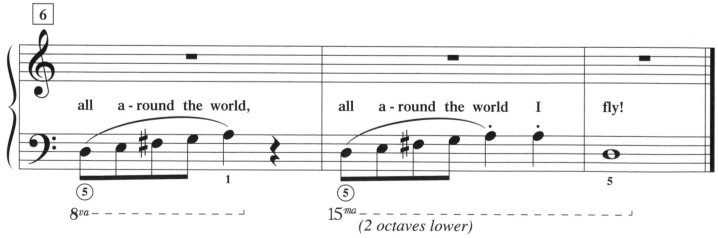

all a-round the world, all a-round the world I fly!

(2 octaves lower)

Note to Teacher: More 5-finger scales are shown at the end of the book (pages 34–39). Students may gradually learn these as they proceed through the book.

Note to Teacher: This piece should be taught by rote.
The student explores the full keyboard range and reviews *tonic* and *dominant* in D, G, and C 5-finger scales.

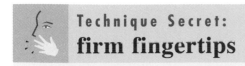

Technique Secret:
firm fingertips

Warm-up with *Finger Inspector* (p. 2).

This piece uses **tonic** and **dominant** notes moving up the keyboard. Have fun with hand crossings!

• Begin crossing the L.H. over while the R.H. is playing.

Hold the damper pedal down throughout the piece.

The Lion's Kingdom
D 5-Finger Scale

Powerful and steady

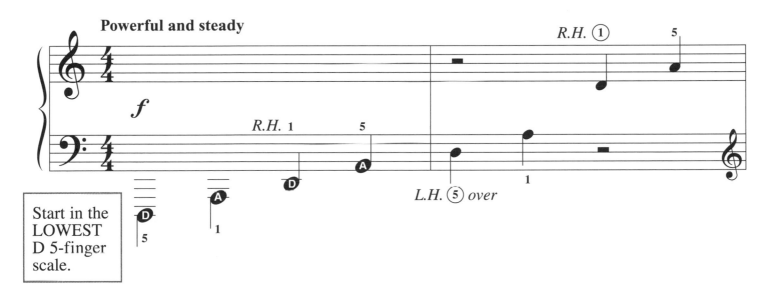

Start in the LOWEST D 5-finger scale.

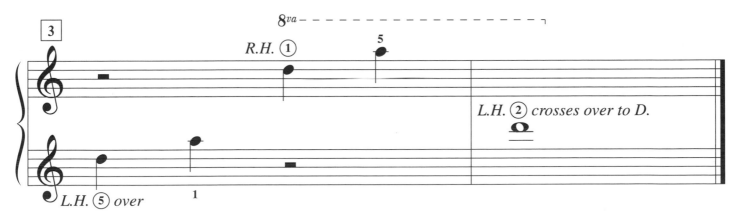

Transpose *The Lion's Kingdom* to the **C 5-finger scale** and **G 5-finger scale**.

melody — the tune

harmony — intervals and chords that are played with the melody

Artistry Hint: Play the **melody** louder than the **harmony**.

Spotlight Tips

- First, play the R.H. alone with a full *mf* tone.

- Then add the L.H. intervals, playing *lightly*. Stay close to the keys.

Spotlight on the Right Hand

_____ 5-Finger Scale

Cheerfully

McArthur, R. Faber

Transpose to the **G 5-finger scale**.

📖 Lesson p.40 (The Queen's Royal Entrance)

- In this piece, which hand plays the **melody**? _____
- Which hand plays the **harmony**? _____

Spotlight Tips

- First, play the L.H. alone with a full *mf* tone.
- Next add the R.H. intervals, playing *lightly*. Stay close to the keys.

Spotlight on the Left Hand

_____ **5-Finger Scale**

McArthur, R. Faber

Transpose to the **C 5-finger scale**.

 Technique Secret:
fast fingers

Warm-up with *Flying Fingers* (p. 3) on the closed keyboard lid.

• Use this finger pattern:

‖: 3 - 4 - 5 - 3 - 2 - 3 - 4 *hold* :‖   "Play" 4 times SLOWLY.
"Play" 4 times QUICKLY.

These exercises use a 4-note pattern.

• Think "step-ping skip-ping" for each pattern.

Finger Olympics
A 5-Finger Scale

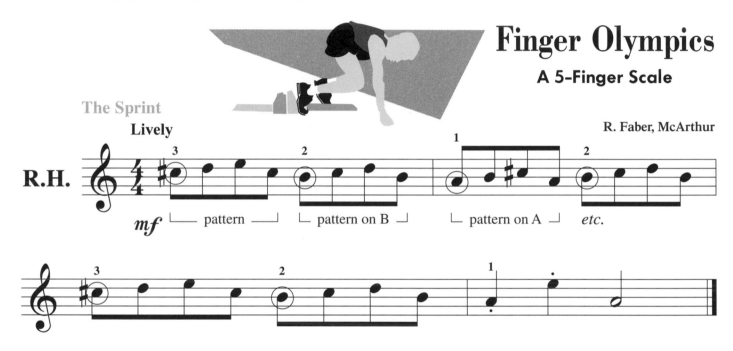

The Sprint

Lively

R. Faber, McArthur

R.H.

mf   pattern   pattern on B   pattern on A   *etc.*

The Hurdles

Lively

pattern   pattern on D   pattern on E   *etc.*

L.H.

mf

 Transpose each exercise to the **D 5-finger scale**.

Warm-up with *Moon Walk* (p. 3) on A's.

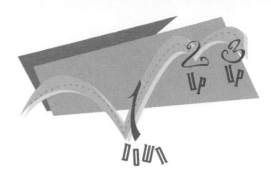

• While playing this waltz, let your
  wrist rise *slightly* as you play finger 3.

Down-Up Waltz

_____5-Finger Scale

Down - up, bounce, Down - up, bounce, waltz - ing a - long.

(prepare L.H.)

5

Down - up, bounce, Down - up, bounce, waltz - ing a - long.

(Continue with the same *down-up* motion.)

9

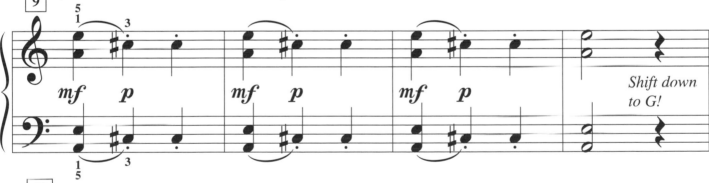

*Shift down
to G!*

13

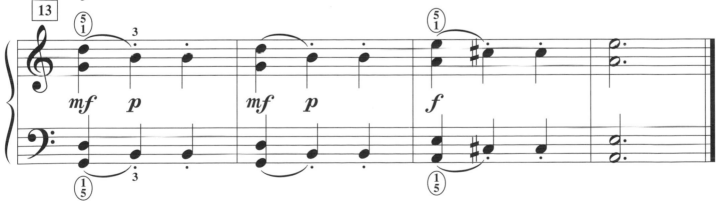

Transpose to the **D 5-finger scale**.

Technique Secret: fast fingers

Warm-up with *Flying Fingers* (p. 3) on the closed keyboard lid.

- Use this finger pattern:

‖: 5 - 3 - 2 - 1 - 5 *hold* :‖

"Play" 4 times SLOWLY.
"Play" 4 times QUICKLY.

This piece uses 3 scale positions: **A**, **D**, and **E**.

- Practice this "boogie bass" until you can move to each scale position with ease.

Hound Dog Boogie
(for L.H. alone)

Note: The teacher may wish to play right-hand A, D, or E chords to accompany the student.

- Can you create a "sound picture" of a hummingbird in spring?
- Circle all the **dynamic markings** before you play. ✎
- Arc your hands playing in **parallel** or **contrary motion**? *(circle)*

Hummingbird Wings

A 5-Finger Scale

N. Faber

Hold the damper pedal down throughout the piece.

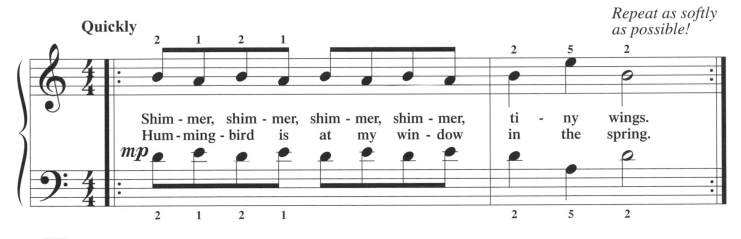

Repeat as softly as possible!

Quickly

Shim - mer, shim - mer, shim - mer, shim - mer, ti - ny wings.
Hum - ming - bird is at my win - dow in the spring.

mp

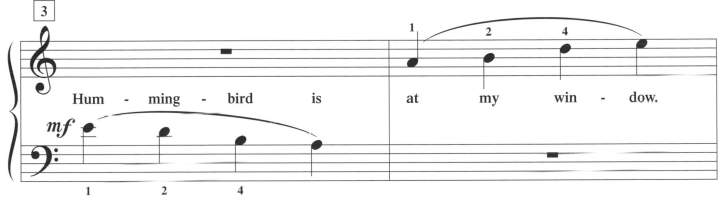

Hum - ming - bird is at my win - dow.

mf

8va¬ Play the highest E on the piano!

Shim - mer, shim - mer, shim - mer, shim - mer, ti - ny wings.

mp

rit.

p

Listen to the shimmer of the hummingbird wings!

This "musical story" of a pirate ship reviews **technique secrets** you have learned.

• Demonstrate each secret for your teacher before playing the music.

Tale of a Pirate Ship

The Captain's Footsteps
D minor

secret: **firm fingertips**

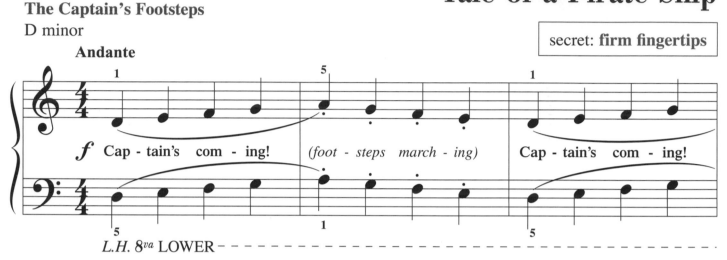

Andante

f Cap - tain's com - ing! *(foot - steps march - ing)* Cap - tain's com - ing!

L.H. 8va LOWER - - - - -

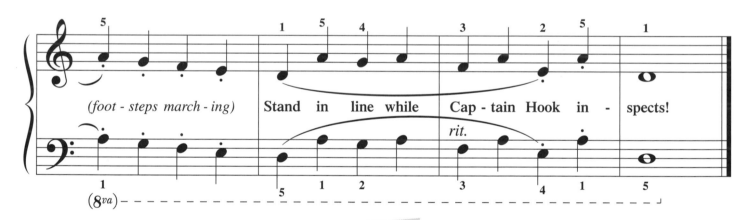

(foot - steps march - ing) Stand in line while Cap - tain Hook in - spects!

rit.

(8va) - - - - -

Stowaway in a Barrel
G minor

Allegro

secret: **light thumb**

p Hid - ing in the ap - ple bar - rel; hope they do not find me sleep - ing here.

• Which exercise above is in **parallel motion**? Which is in **contrary motion**?

Counting the Jewels
A minor

secret: **hands-together coordination**

Moderato

Count - ing   all   my   gold   and   sil - ver;

I'm   the   rich - est   pi - rate   on   the   sea!

Play the lowest A on the piano!

Storm at Sea
C minor

secret: **wrist float-off**

Allegro

Float - off,   high   winds,   float - off,   soaring,

float - off,   storm   at   sea!

Play the lowest C on the piano!

Technique Secret:
hands-together coordination

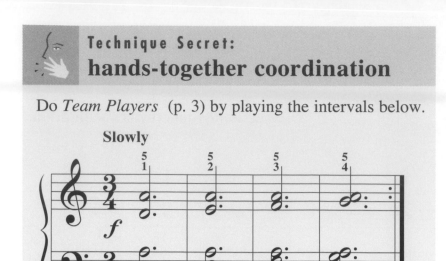

Do *Team Players* (p. 3) by playing the intervals below.

Slowly

This piece is an **interval study** using a *staccato* touch.

• Watch for the ⟨ and ⟩.

Early America

1. Making Horseshoes

_____ **minor 5-Finger Scale**

Moderato

(hammering the metal)

(fanning the coals)

repeat!

(The flames get hotter and hotter!)

Transpose to the **A minor 5-finger scale**.

- Notice that *The Spinning Wheel* uses the same intervals as in *Making Horseshoes*.

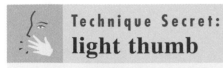

Technique Secret:
light thumb

Warm-up with *Light as a Feather* (p. 2).

Spinning Wheel Tips

- **The circled notes outline the hidden melody.**
  Listen to the melody by first playing only these notes.

- **The repeated A's help create a spinning motion.**
  Play them lightly!

2. The Spinning Wheel

_____ minor 5-Finger Scale

Transpose to the **C minor 5-finger scale**.

Lesson p.50 (Sword Dance)

The malagueña is a colorful Spanish
dance played by guitars and castanets.

• Bring out the exciting **mood** of this piece
  with your fine technique and artistry!

Malagueña

Traditional theme
adapted

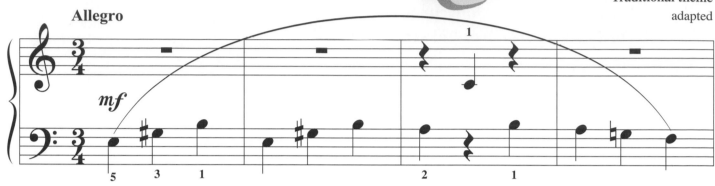

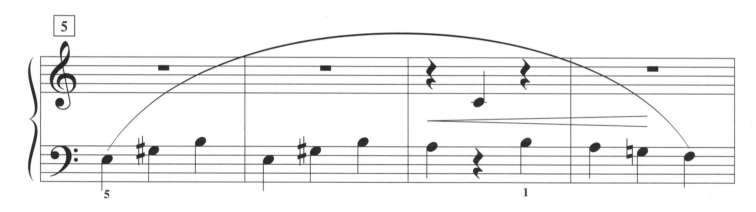

Lesson p.54 (Jazz Blast)

FF1098

Repeat from
measure 13.

Note to Teacher: These pages present the **12 major 5-finger scales** and **7 white-key minor 5-finger scales**. They may be taught after p. 26 in the *2A Lesson Book,* or earlier if the teacher prefers.

Major 5-Finger Scales

Whole step - Whole step - Half step - Whole step

Hint: The C, G, and F major chords are all
white-white-white.

Write your initials in each blank when you have learned and memorized these positions.

C Major

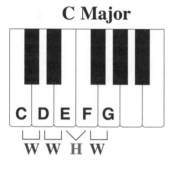

C D E F G
W W H W

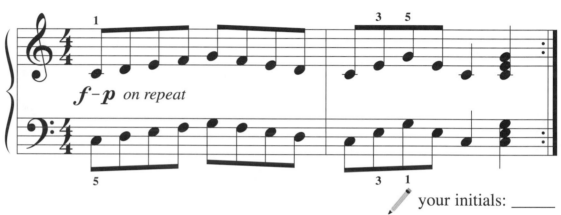

f-p on repeat

✏ your initials: _____

G Major

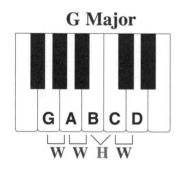

G A B C D
W W H W

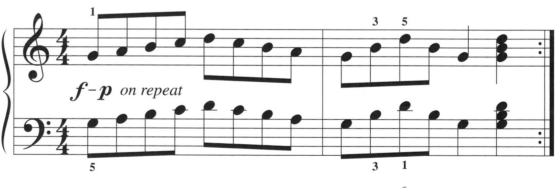

f-p on repeat

✏ your initials: _____

F Major

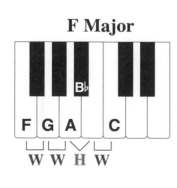

F G A C
Bb
W W H W

f-p on repeat

✏ your initials: _____

Note to Teacher: To enhance visual learning, accidentals are re-written within the measure for the major chords.

Hint: The D, A, and E major chords are all
white-black-white.

D Major

f-p on repeat

🖉 your initials: _____

A Major

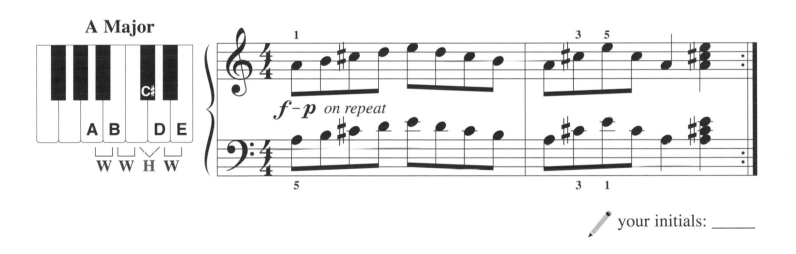

f-p on repeat

🖉 your initials: _____

E Major

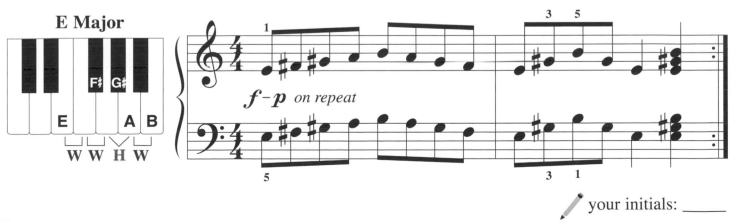

f-p on repeat

🖉 your initials: _____

Hint: The D♭, A♭, and E♭ major chords are all

black-white-black.

D♭ Major

f-*p* on repeat

your initials: _____

A♭ Major

f-*p* on repeat

your initials: _____

E♭ Major

f-*p* on repeat

your initials: _____

FF1098

Hint: The major scales and chords for B, Bb, and Gb (or F#) are all different.

- Memorize the unique patterns of these major 5-finger scales and chords.

B Major

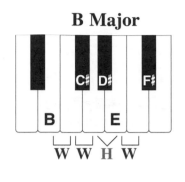

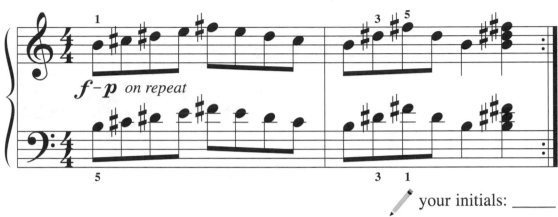

f-p on repeat

your initials: _____

Bb Major

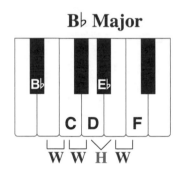

f-p on repeat

your initials: _____

Gb Major

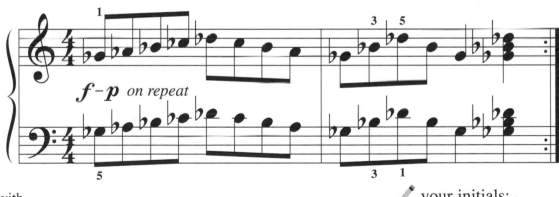

f-p on repeat

This scale can be written with flats or sharps.

your initials: _____

F# Major

f-p on repeat

your initials: _____

Note to Teacher: Following are the **minor 5-finger scales** that begin on white keys.
They may be taught after p. 40 in the *2A Lesson Book*.

Minor 5-Finger Scales

Whole step - Half step - Whole step - Whole step

Hint: The C minor, G minor, and F minor chords are all

white-black-white.

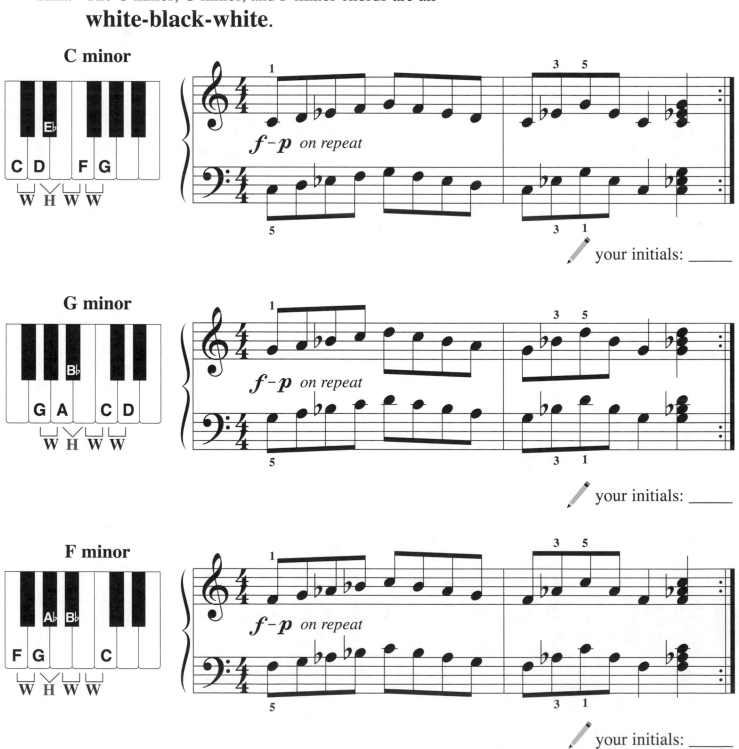

your initials: _____

your initials: _____

your initials: _____

FF1098

Hint: The D minor, A minor, and E minor chords are all **white-white-white**.

For all 12 minor 5-finger patterns, see
Achievement Skill Sheet No. 2, Minor 5-Finger Patterns and Cross-Hand Arpeggios (AS5002).

Certificate of Fabulous Fingers

Congratulations to:

_____

(Your Name)

You have completed LEVEL 2A TECHNIQUE & ARTISTRY

and are now ready for LEVEL 2B

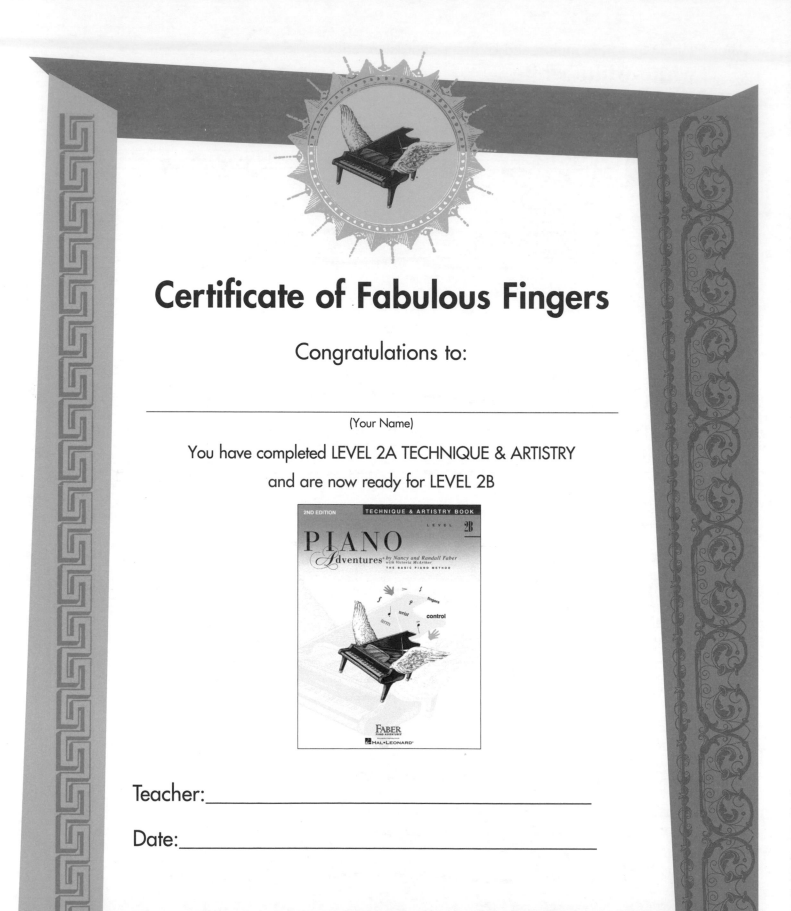

Teacher:_____

Date:_____